Department of the Interior

Aviation Life Support Equipment

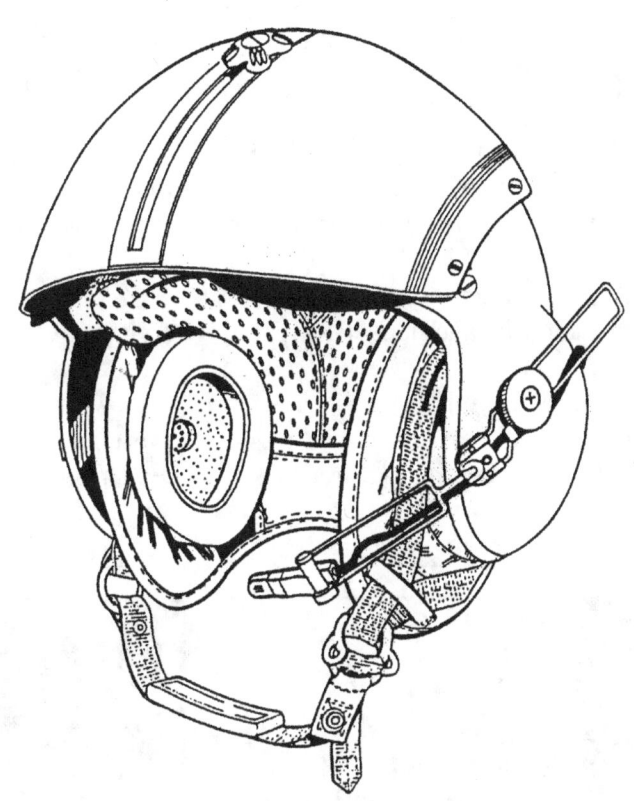

Flight Helmet User's Guide

June 2008

The requirement for flight helmets and other aviation life support equipment (ALSE) begins in 351 DM 1 and expanded information is found in the DOI ALSE Handbook, which can be downloaded at (http://amd.nbc.gov/safety/library/Alsehb.PDF).

This DOI Flight Helmet User's Guide is intended to inform and assist aviation personnel in the proper wear, care, and maintenance of their flight helmet and can be downloaded at (http://amd.nbc.gov/safety/library/helmetguide.pdf).

The proper donning and doffing procedures for the SPH-5 flight helmet are explained in an Interagency Aviation Video Safety Alert (http://amd.nbc.gov/safety/vid-library.htm).

An excellent article describing how to wear and care for your flight helmet can be found in the January 2005 edition of the Army's Flightfax magazine (see pages 12-13) (https://crc.army.mil/MediaAndPubs/magazines/flightfax/2005_issues/ffjan05.pdf).

The user of the flight helmet is responsible to ensure that the helmet is serviceable before flight. If your flight helmet requires repair or evaluation by a technically qualified person you should first refer to your Bureau's policy, and then if appropriate contact either:

1. Bureau Aviation Safety Specialist.
2. Bureau of Land Management (BLM) Ramp Services, in Boise, Idaho (208) 387-5529.

Technicians at the BLM Ramp Services can support users with special needs such as military avionics (earphones and microphones) and requests to install items such as coiled cords, extensions, and adapters when inter-Bureau fiscal agreements have been established.

Document Approving Authority and Custodian

	351 DM 1 352 DM 1 ALSE Handbook	*Mark L. Bathrick* (signature)
Effective Date:	06/10/2008	
Expiration Date:	Not applicable	**Mark L. Bathrick**
Document Custodian:	NBC AMD Aviation Safety and Program Evaluation Manager	**Associate Director AMD**

Revision History

07/14/2005	1.01	Initial release	Robert Galloway
06/10/2008	1.02	Addition of document approving authority, review, and revision tables.	Robert Galloway

Investigations over the past several years have consistently proven the value of flight helmets in airplane and helicopter accidents.

Two rotor blade strikes to the helmet… No permanent head injuries.

Aircraft impacted inverted and seatbelt failed… No head injuries to the survivor.

After impact the airplane rotated 180°… No head injuries.

Aircraft impacted on left side after 100' fall… No serious head injuries to the survivors.

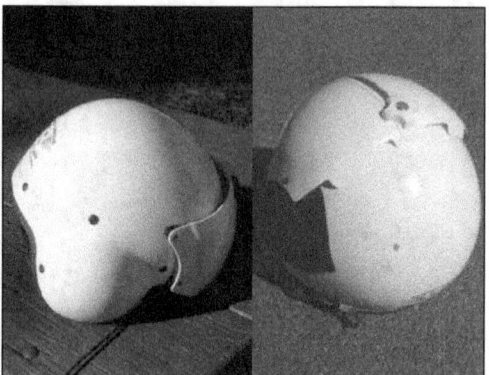

Aircraft impacted on left side… No head injuries.

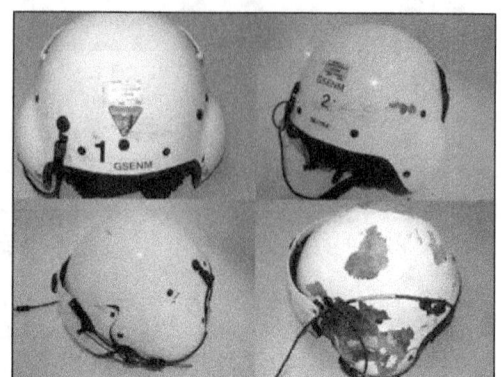

Main rotor blade struck 4 passenger's helmets… Only one serious injury.

Will your flight helmet be ready to protect you when the time comes ?

INSPECTIONS

Inspections consist of pre- and post-flight inspections by the user, periodic/annual inspections by a "properly trained" person, and special inspections by a "technically qualified" person.

> *Users* should familiarize themselves with the serviceability and inspection criteria found in this Guide and their respective flight helmets' manual.

> A "*properly trained*" person shall have completed hands-on training for periodic/annual inspections under the supervision of a "technically qualified" person.

> A "*technically qualified*" person shall have completed hands-on training in the disassembly, inspection, repair, and reassembly of flight helmets. Acceptable training may be received from flight helmet manufacturers, military, or other organizations that regularly inspect and repair flight helmets.

The following inspection criteria has been adapted from the Gentex SPH-5 helmet manual (http://www.gentexcorp.com/PDFfiles/TechPubs/SPH-5%20Single%20Visor%20(TP0056r7).pdf)

Preflight Inspection. Prior to each flight, the *user* should inspect the helmet assembly to see that it is serviceable and in good working order using table 1. This inspection should ensure that:

1. The helmet, liners and earcup assemblies have been fitted properly.
2. The chinstrap and nape strap are adjusted properly and the retention assembly is attached to the helmet with the screws tightened securely.
3. The visor(s) operate properly and are clean and free of cracks or scratches.
4. All communication components are properly installed and the earphones and microphone operate properly.
5. The overall condition of the helmet has been checked for serviceability.

Postflight Inspection. After each flight, the *user* should note any component malfunction or damage to the helmet resulting from operational use. Affected components should be replaced (see the specific helmet's manual).

Periodic Inspection. Users are responsible for ensuring that their helmet is clean and that all components are working properly. Periodic (scheduled) inspections should be conducted at a minimum of annually or as required by a *properly trained* person.

Special Inspection. A *technically qualified* person will evaluate any government-owned flight helmet that is suspected of having been subjected to impact (i.e. hit by a rock or dropped), or other potentially damaging event. Following an aircraft accident or incident-with-potential the NBC AMD Investigator-in-Charge will determine if the flight helmets involved require a special inspection.

Pre- and post-flight inspection checklist

COMPONENT	INSPECT FOR:
Helmet Shell	Cracks, holes, warping. Cleanliness.
Energy-Absorbing Liner	Worn or loose hook fasteners. Gouges, cracks, indentations.
Thermo-Plastic Liner (TPL)	Torn or damaged areas. Loose bond at edges. Worn cover.
Earcup Assembly	Cracked cup, broken or missing tab, torn earseal, worn earphone holder or spacer pad, or failed earphone. Cleanliness.
Retention Assembly (including nape strap and chinstrap)	Frayed or torn fabric, loose stitching, corroded or bent buckles or snap. Cleanliness.
Microphone, Boom, Cord, Swivel Assembly	Failed microphone; damaged or worn swivel or boom; damaged cord.
Communications Cord	Cuts, cracks, deteriorated insulation, general damage.
Visor Assembly	Cracks, scratches, loose knobs. Cleanliness.

Table 1

EXAMPLES

Photos with red borders show deficiencies that ground the helmet and require repair before use.

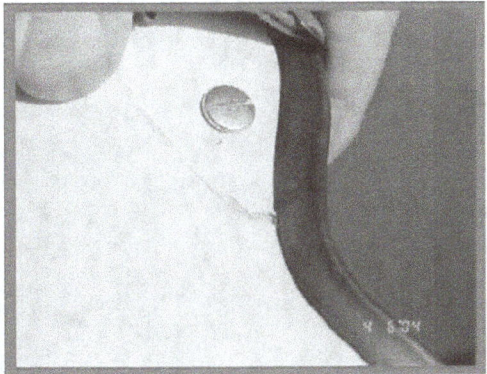

Photos with yellow borders show deficiencies that should be repaired as soon as possible

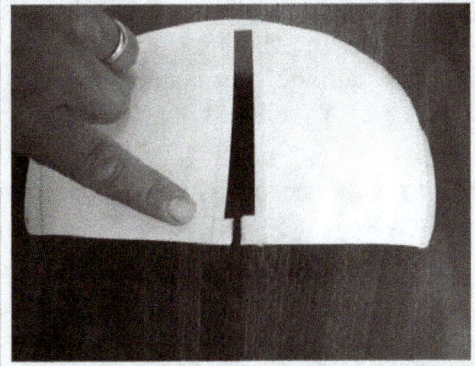

Photos with green borders show helmet parts that are available through the NWCG National Fire Equipment System Catalog.

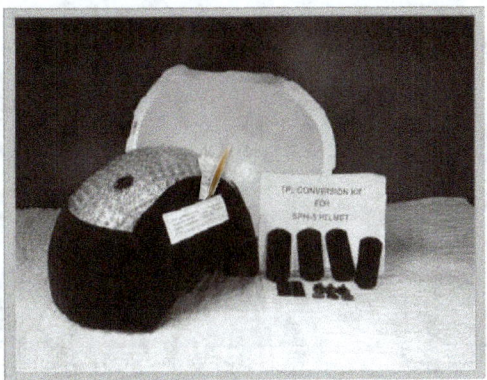

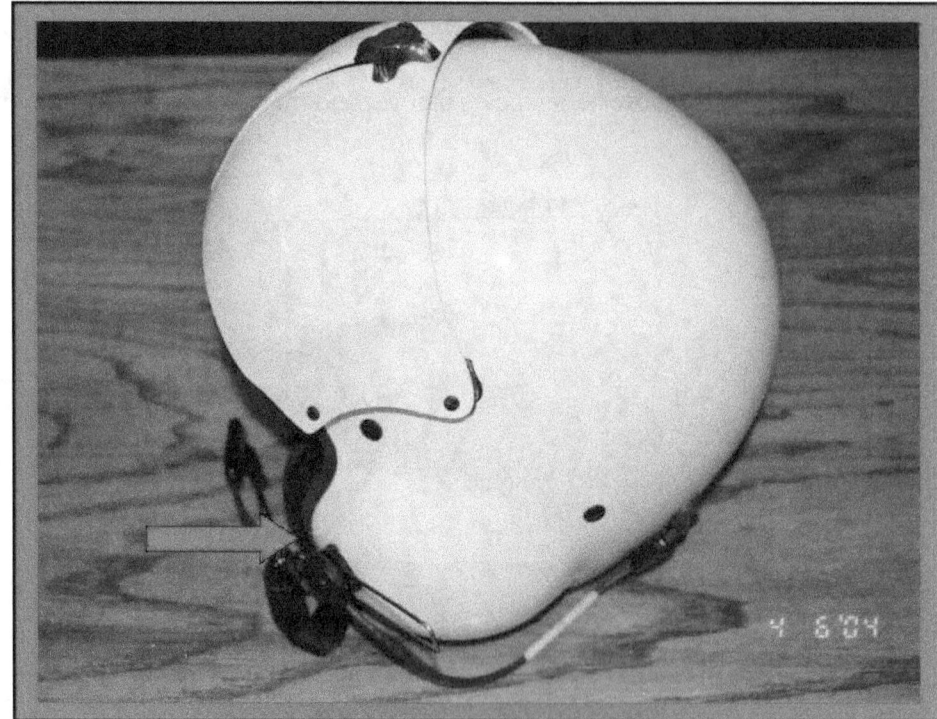

Misuse of the helmet often causes the shell to crack on the forward and rear edges of the ear cup. Excessive spreading may damage your helmet. Spread the helmet just enough to allow ease of donning.

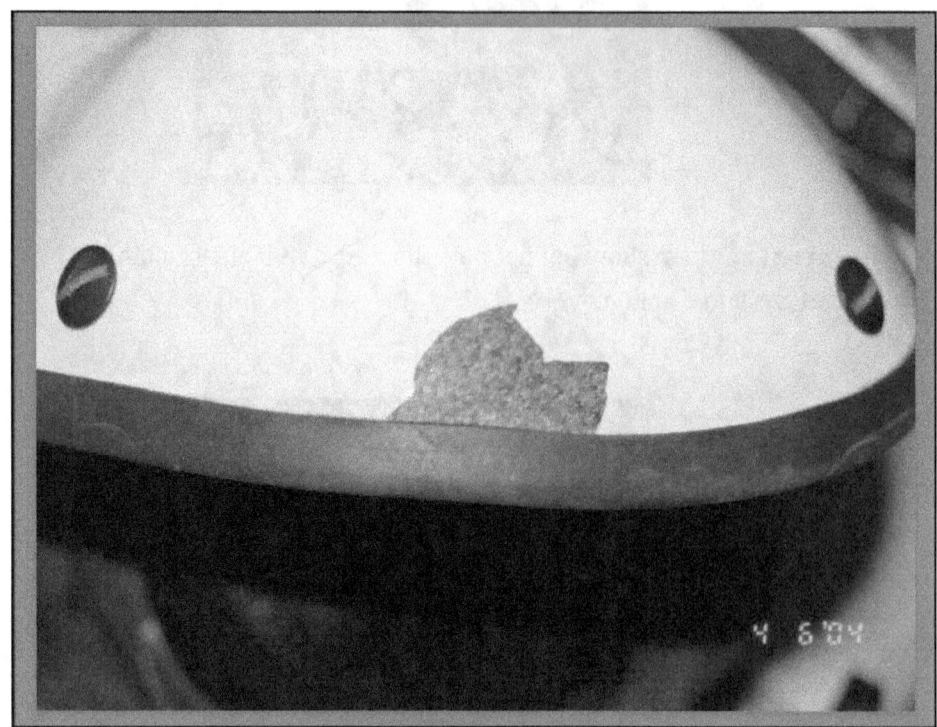

Chipped, cracked, or missing paint may indicate an underlying crack, but how would you know for sure?

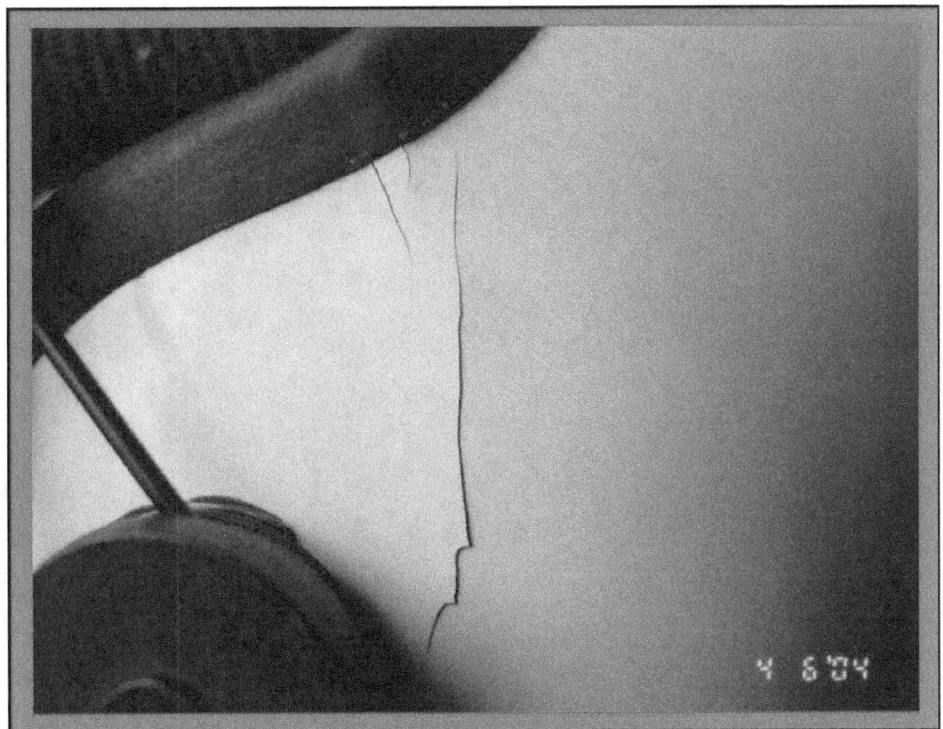

Are these cracks in the paint or cracks in the shell?... Do you know for sure?...
Send it in and have it checked!

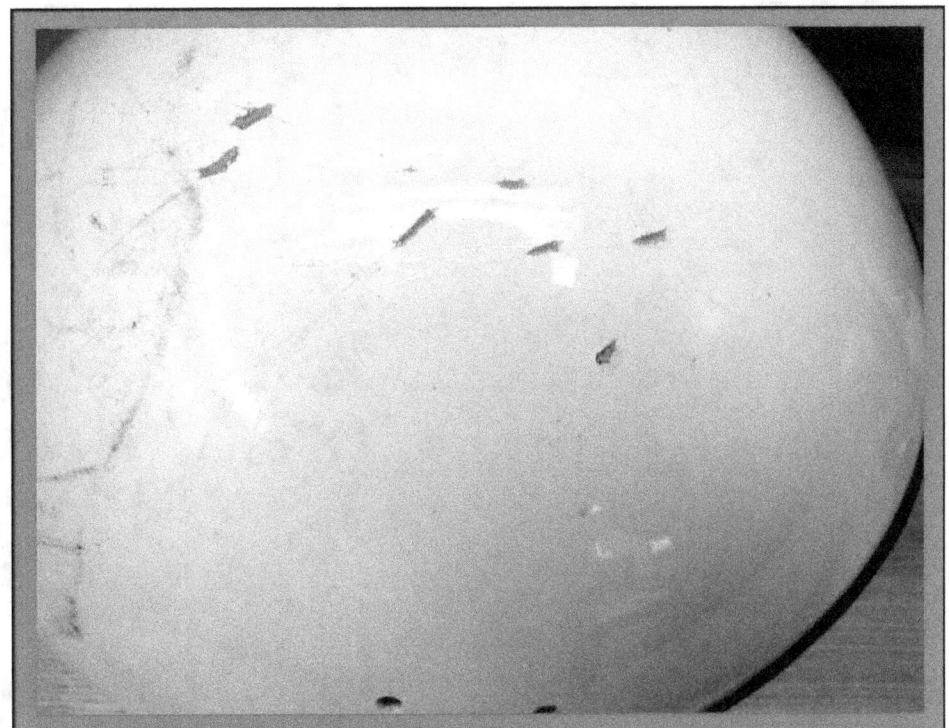

Nicks and gouges in the shell can compromise the shells strength and integrity.
This may be from misuse or previous damage. Have it checked.

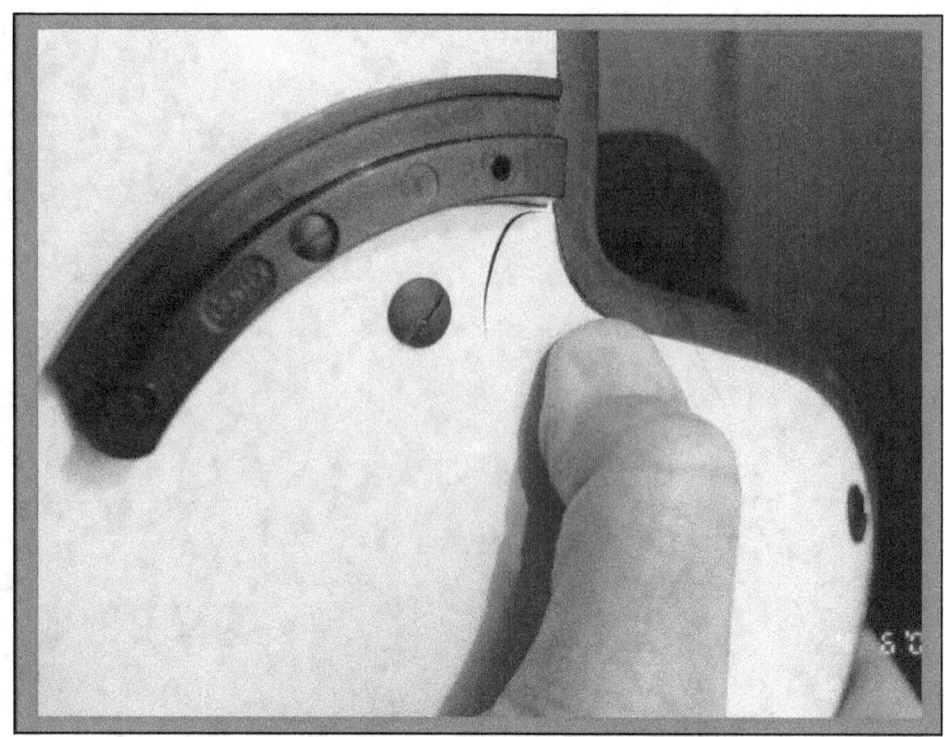

Helmet cracks often occur around the ear cup.
A crack or other serious damage to a helmet's shell makes the helmet unserviceable.

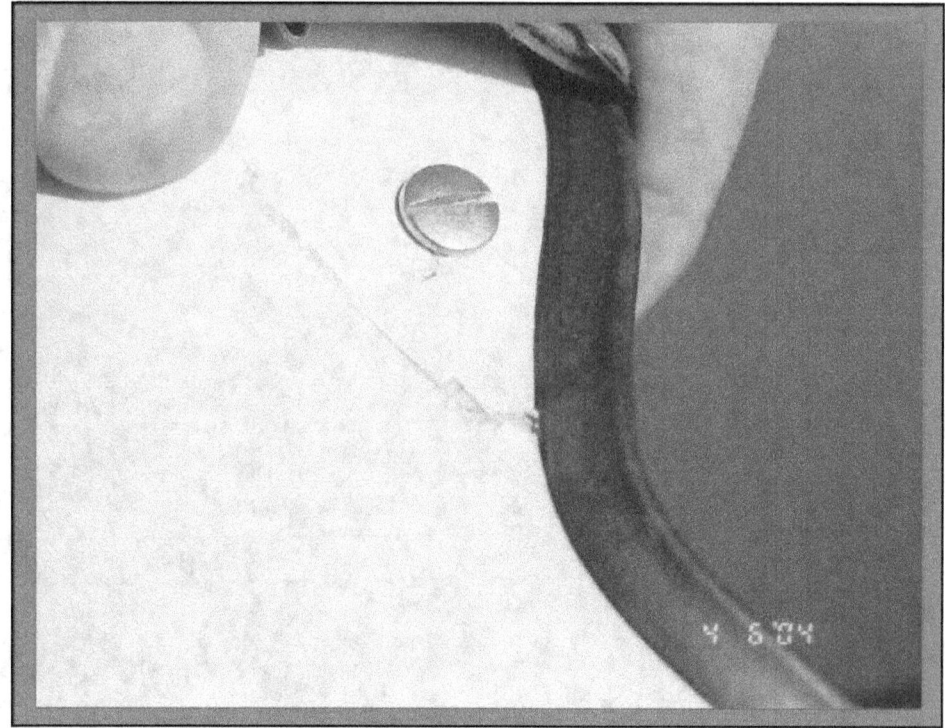

Some cracks are very noticeable.

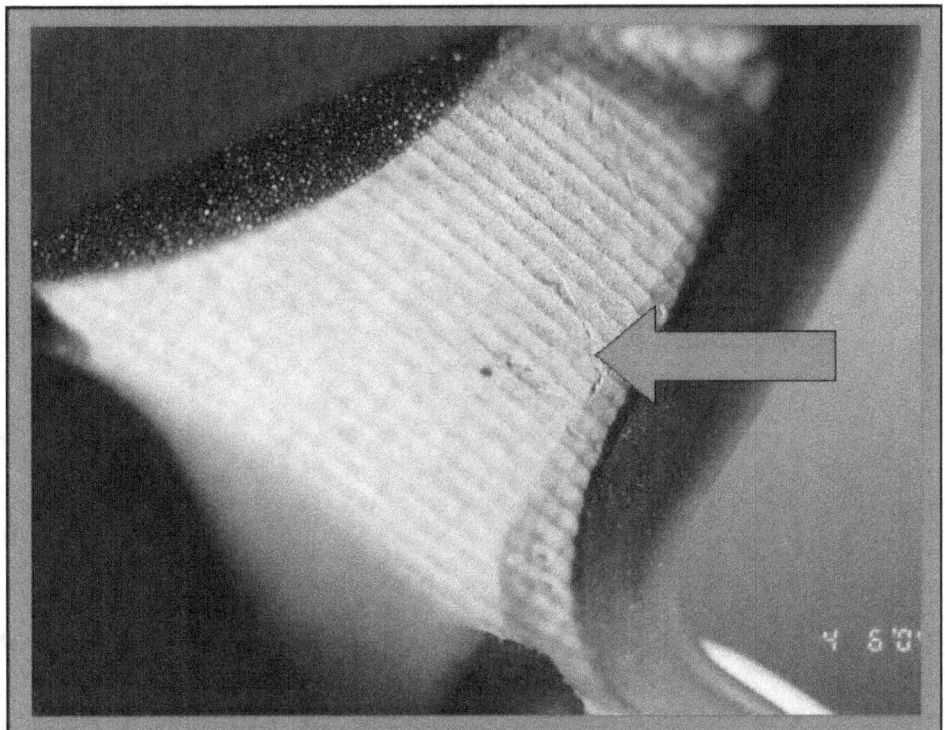

This crack could only be seen from the inside of shell.

Ear cups (hard plastic) that are damaged will take away from side impact integrity and will cause the user pain or discomfort.

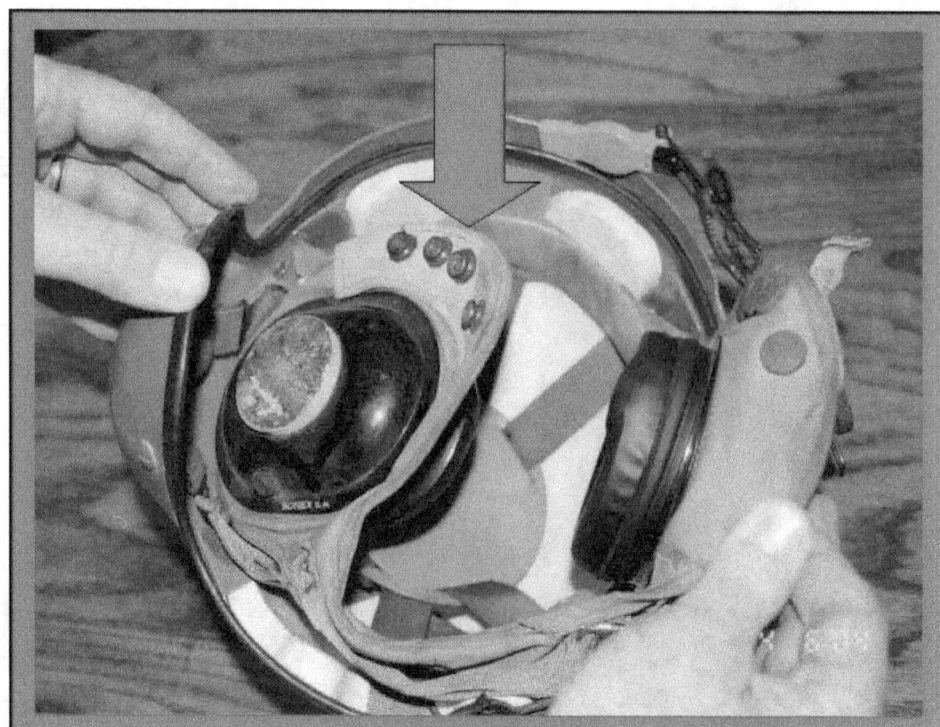

Old style retention assemblies with leather reinforcements need to be replaced.
This type of retention assembly does not meet current standards.

Do not use rivets to install identification tags to helmets because rivets cause damage to the
shell and can hide cracks. Similarly, paint and adhesive stickers can hide cracks and should
be only used on the helmet's visor cover, not on the helmet's shell.

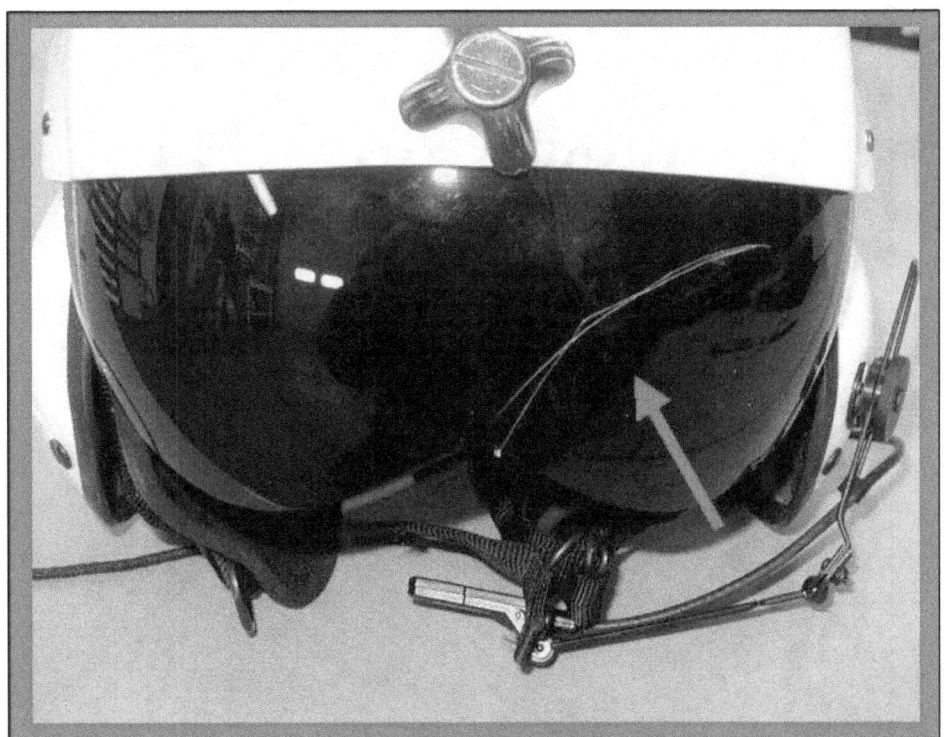

Replace your visor if it has cracks or other damage (scratches or abrasion) that interferes with your ability to see clearly.

Deep dents or gouges to, or pieces missing from the Styrofoam make the liner unserviceable.

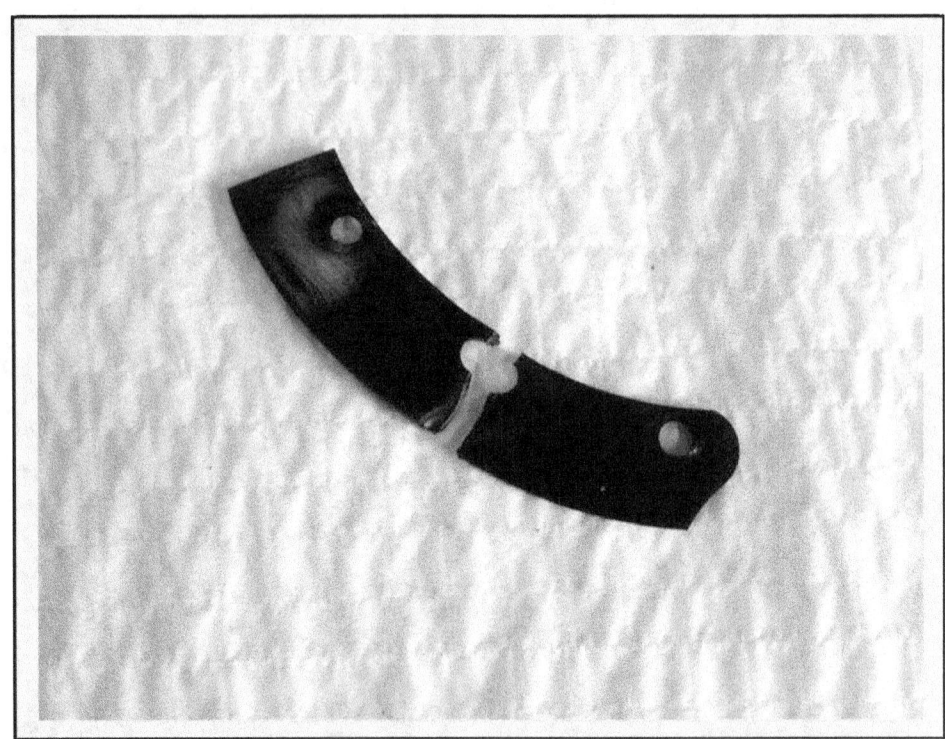

Broken visor tracks will make it difficult to operate your visor.
Replace as soon as possible.

Cracked or broken visor housings make it difficult to operate your visor.
Replace as soon as possible.

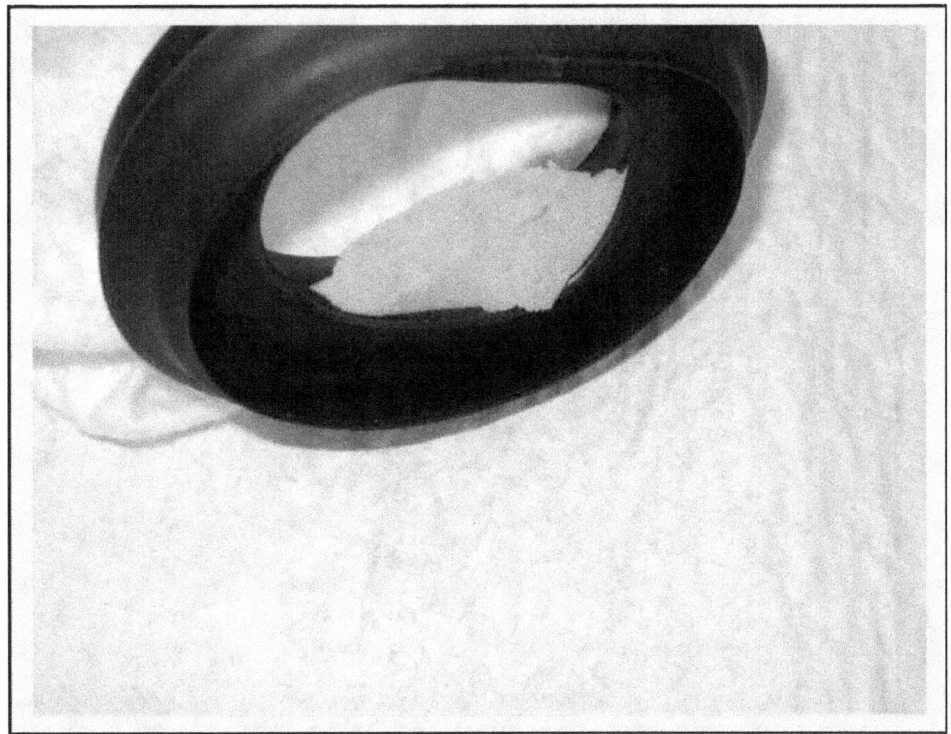

Ear seals (soft plastic) that are ripped or are no longer pliable will cause you discomfort and increase noise. Replace as soon as possible.

Proper fitting cannot be achieved with broken, frayed or missing tension straps. Tension straps with no elasticity also need to be replaced as soon as possible.

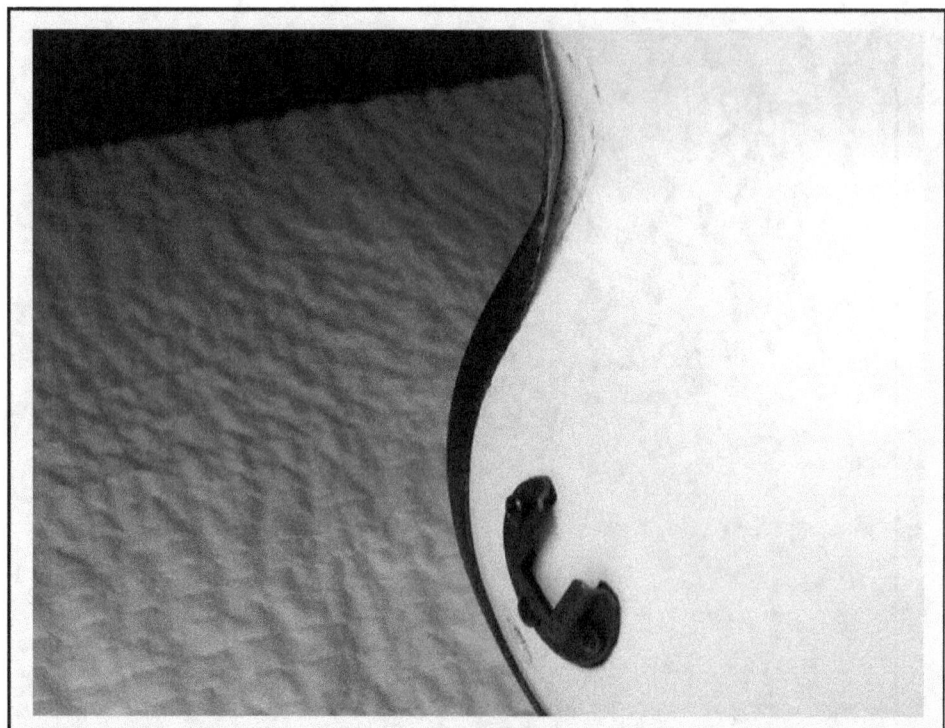

Loose beading can be glued down using contact cement - repair as soon as possible.
Missing or torn beading exposes the outer edge of helmet to damage - replace ASAP.

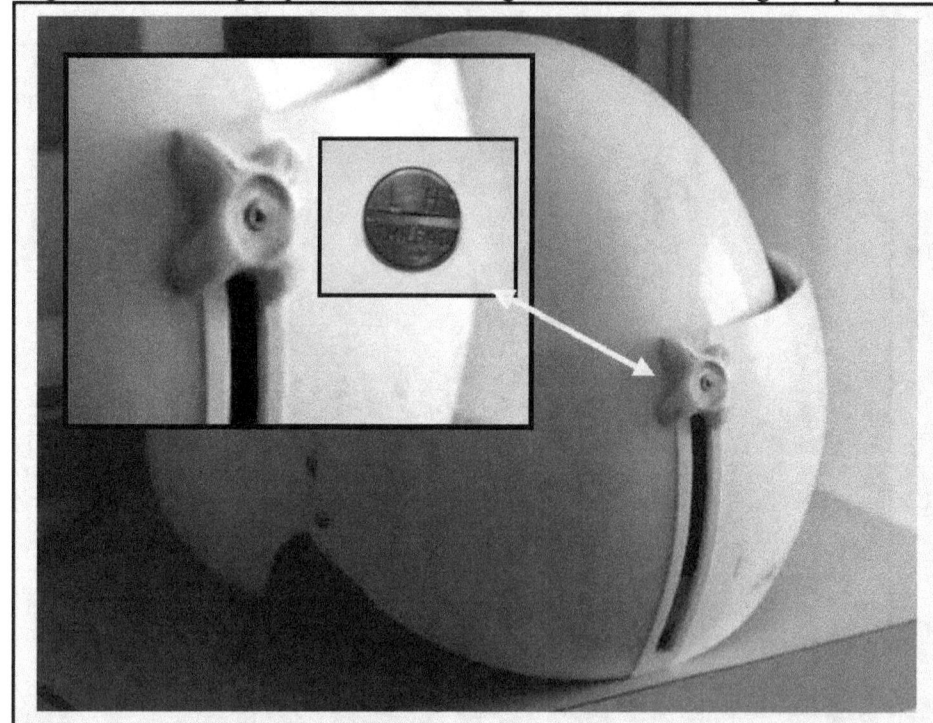

Without the visor retaining screw the knob can back off and make securing the visor
impossible. Have it replaced as soon as possible.
NOTE: The retaining screw has a left hand thread. A full visor lock assembly must be
ordered to replace a missing retaining screw.

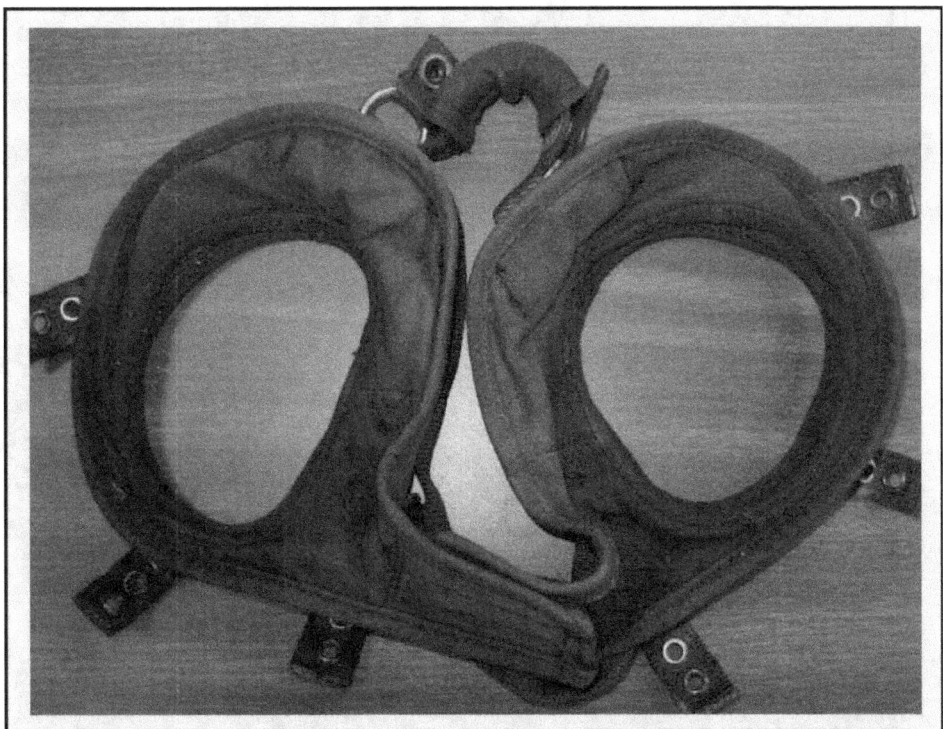

Heavily soiled retention assemblies become stiff and non-pliable.
Replace as soon as possible.

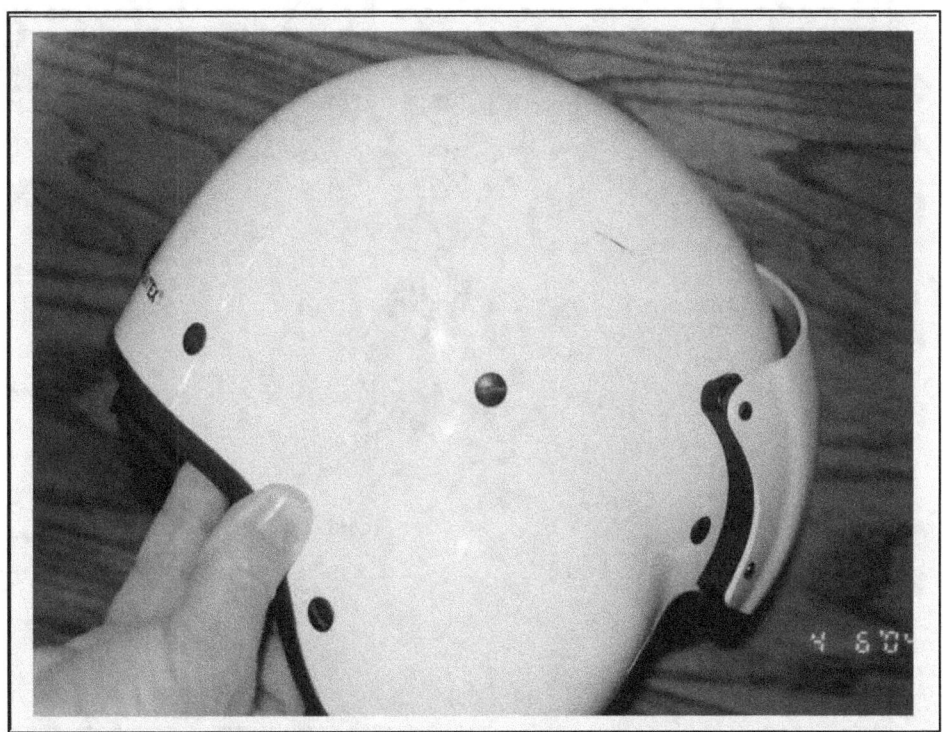

Minor scuffs and scratches will happen with normal use.
Look for cracks and gouges and loose hardware before each mission. If you are not sure have it checked.

Ear cup chaffing pads should be intact and pliable.
If they deteriorate – replace as soon as possible.

Frayed casings for microphone cords can allow the cord to become damaged.
Replace as soon as possible.

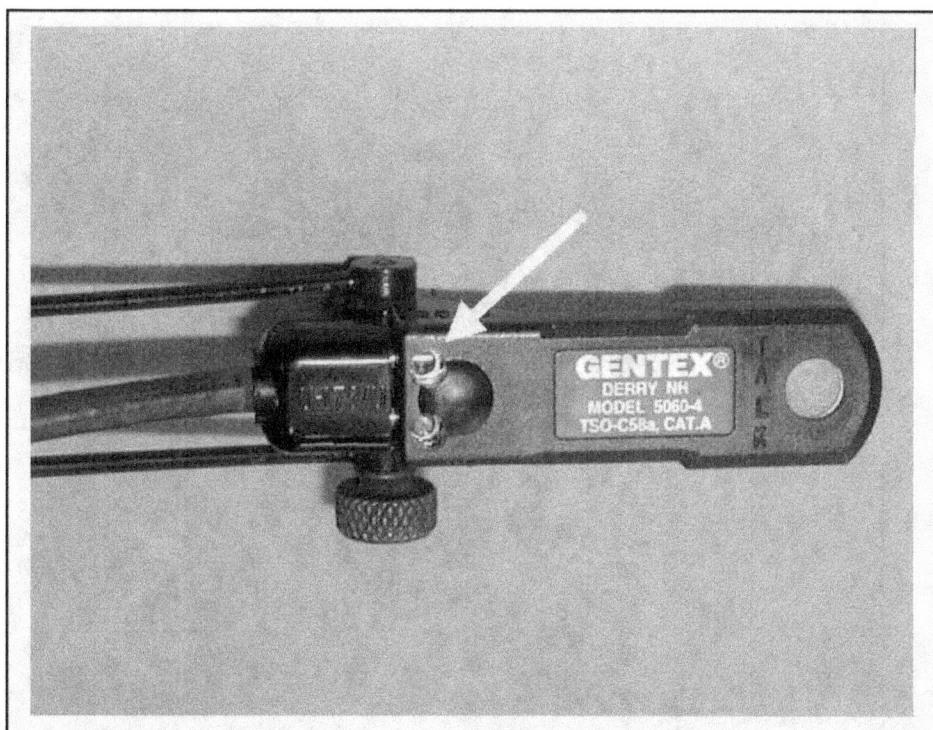

Check for loose or missing microphone screws.

If your ear phone is loose or the foam ear cup pads are deteriorated have them checked as soon as possible

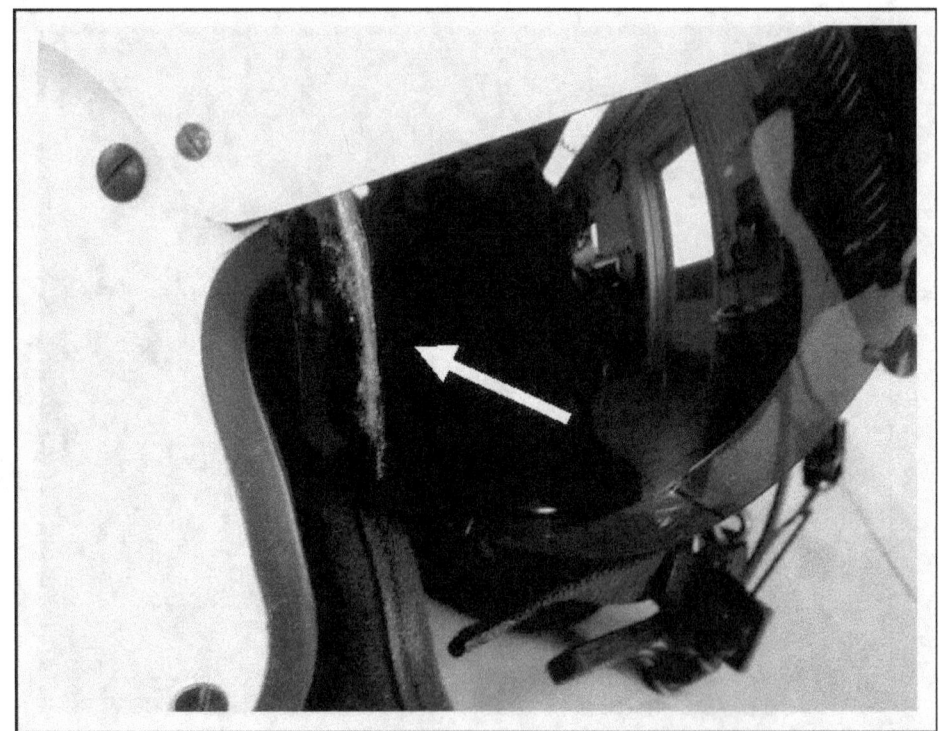

Abrasions on the side of the visor are OK as long as they don't interfere with your vision.

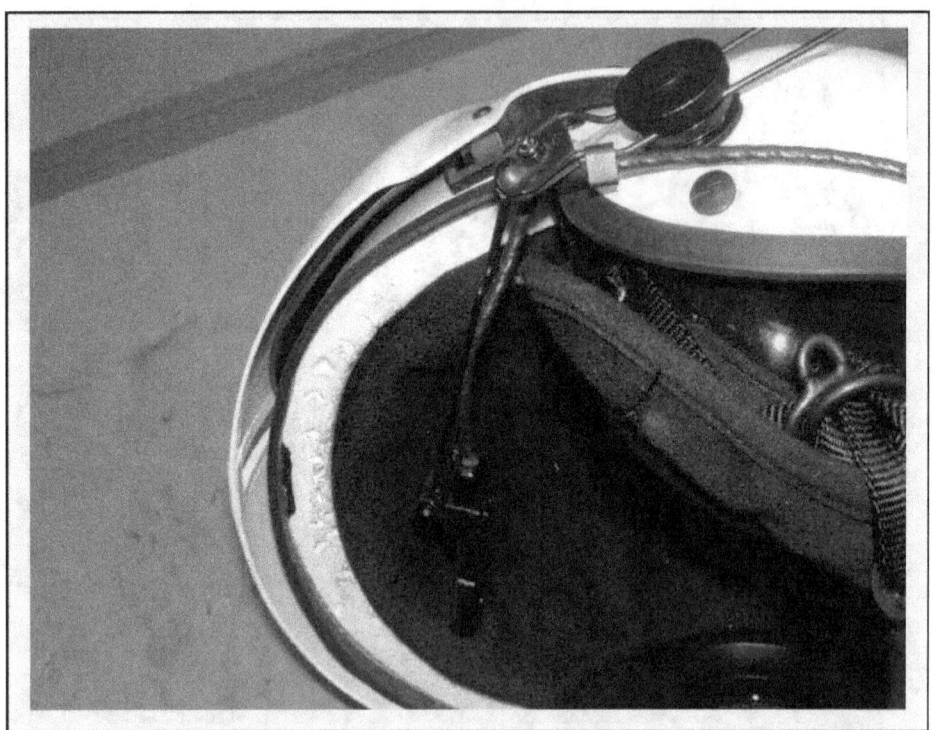

Minor indentations or scratches to the Styrofoam liner are OK.

Parts to fix your helmet in the NWCG National Fire Equipment System Catalog.

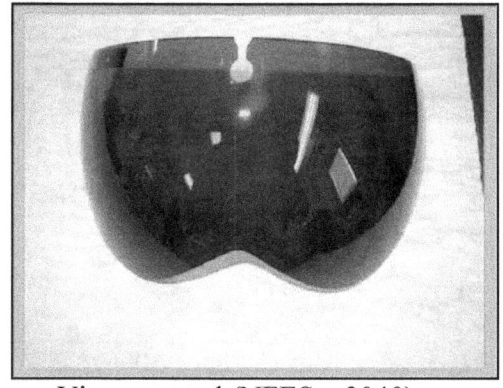

Visor, neutral (NFES – 3040)

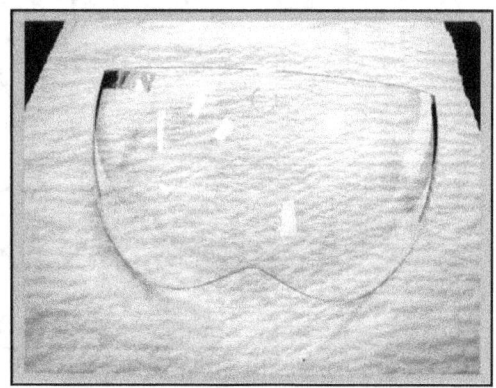

Visor, clear (NFES – 3039)

Visor, Housing (NFES – 3042)

Track, visor, left, black (NFES – 3050)
Track, visor, right, black (NFES – 3051)

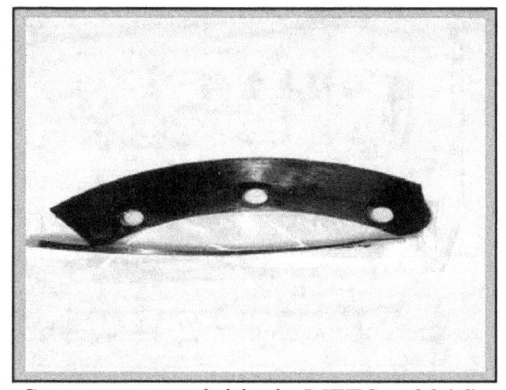

Spacer, tapered, black (NFES – 3046)

Spacer, visor (NFES – 3052)

Parts to fix your helmet in the NWCG National Fire Equipment System Catalog.

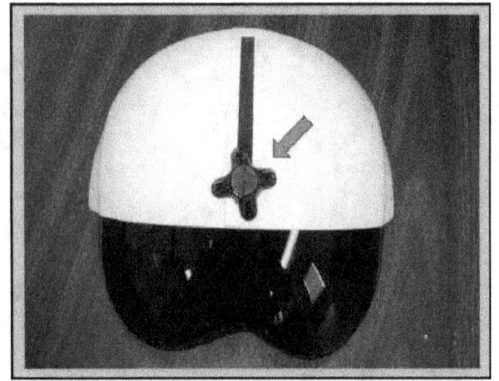

Visor, lock assembly, black (NFES – 3041)

Ear seals (NFES – 3056)

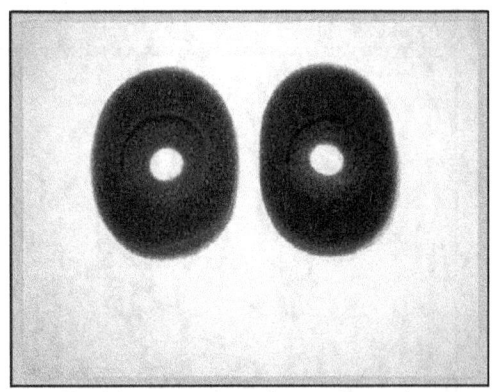

Cushion, ear cup insert Part-A
(NFES – 3057)

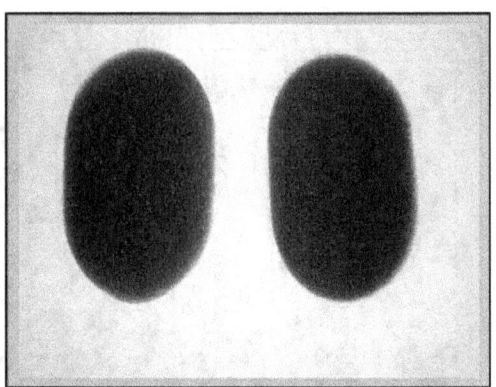

Cushion, ear cup insert Part-B
(NFES – 3058)

Earphone 600 Ohm (NFES – 3069)

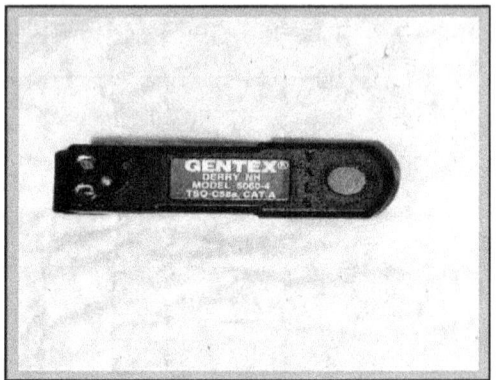

Microphone element (NFES – 3025)

Parts to fix your helmet in the NWCG National Fire Equipment System Catalog.

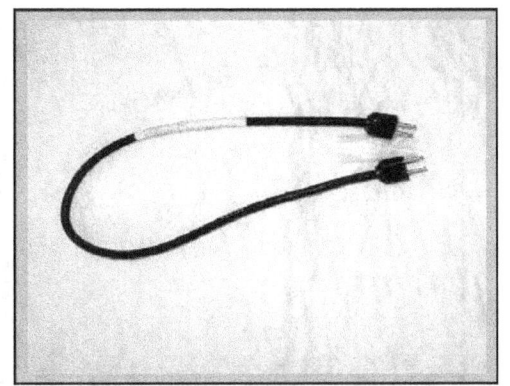

Cable assembly, microphone (NFES – 3024)

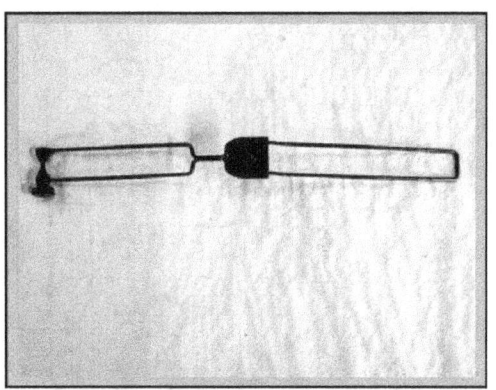

Boom assembly (NFES – 3023)

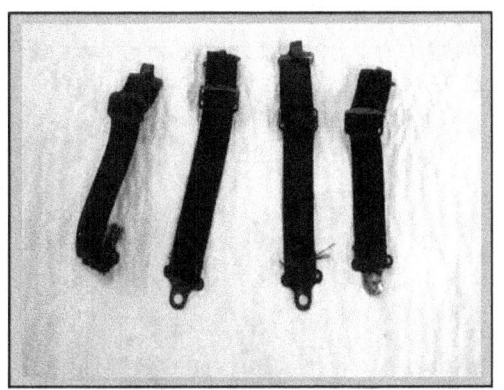

Strap, ear cup tension (NFES – 3053)

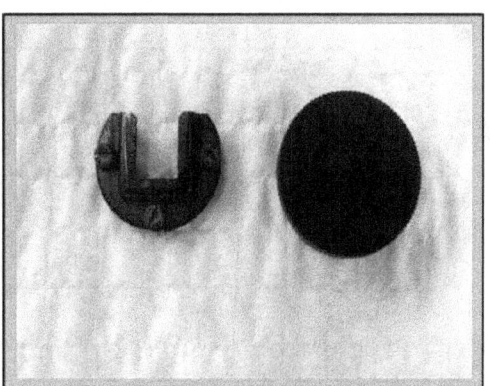

Boom support, low profile
with mounting hardware (NFES – 3071)

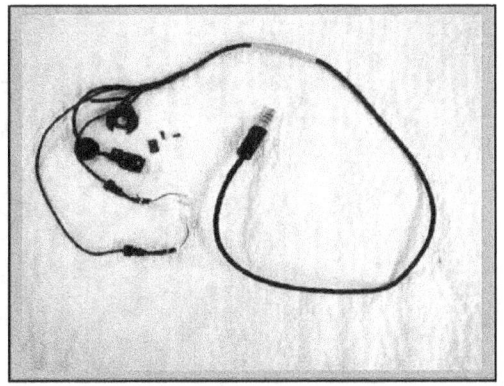

Cord assembly, parallel, single male
(NFES – 3073)

Layer assembly, SPH-5C regular (NFES – 3066)
Layer assembly, SPH-5C XL (NFES – 3067)

Parts to fix your helmet in the NWCG National Fire Equipment System Catalog.

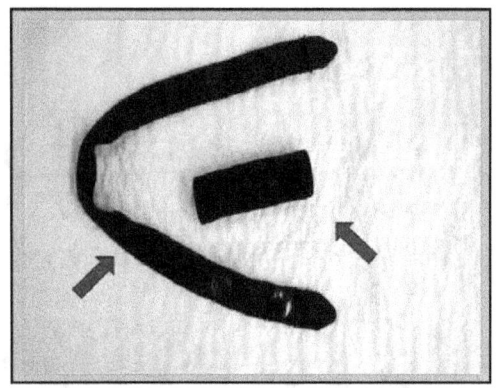

Strap, chin, black (NFES – 3060)
Chinstrap, pad, black (NFES – 3059)

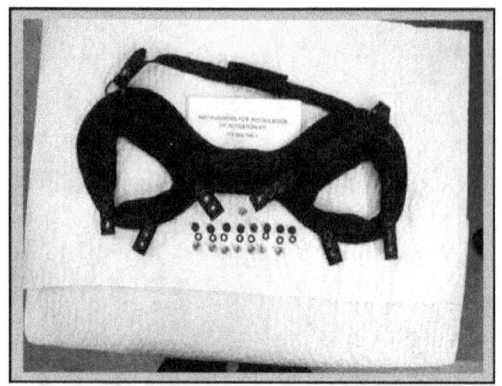

Kit, retrofit, SPH-5C wide yoke retention
(NFES – 3019)

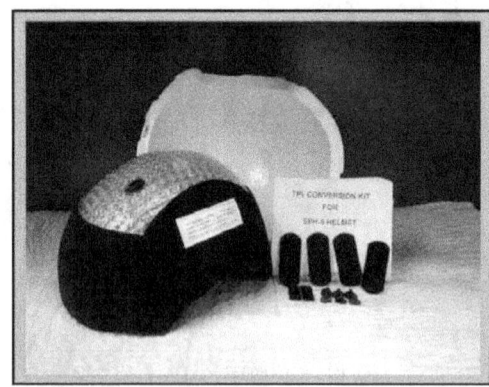

Kit, TPL conversion, Regular (NFES – 3016)
Kit, TPL conversion, XL (NFES – 3017)
Kit, TPL conversion, Small (NFES-3018)

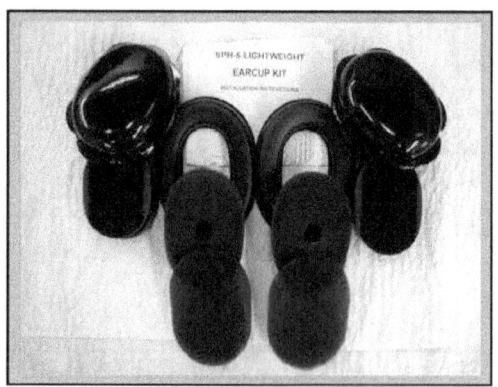

Ear cup set, light weight SPH-5C
(NFES – 3055)

Visor, screw attachment kit (NFES – 3043)

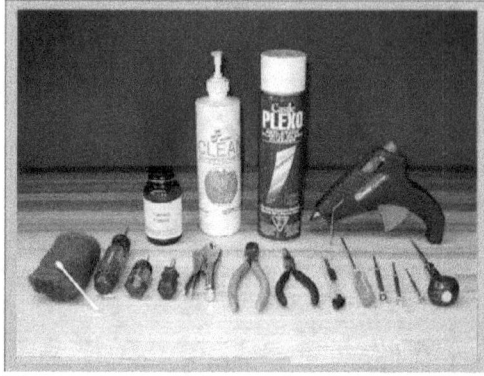

The tools needed to maintain your flight
helmet can be found at a hardware store.

How NOT to treat your flight helmet !!!

A helmet is a high-priced radio, treat it like one.

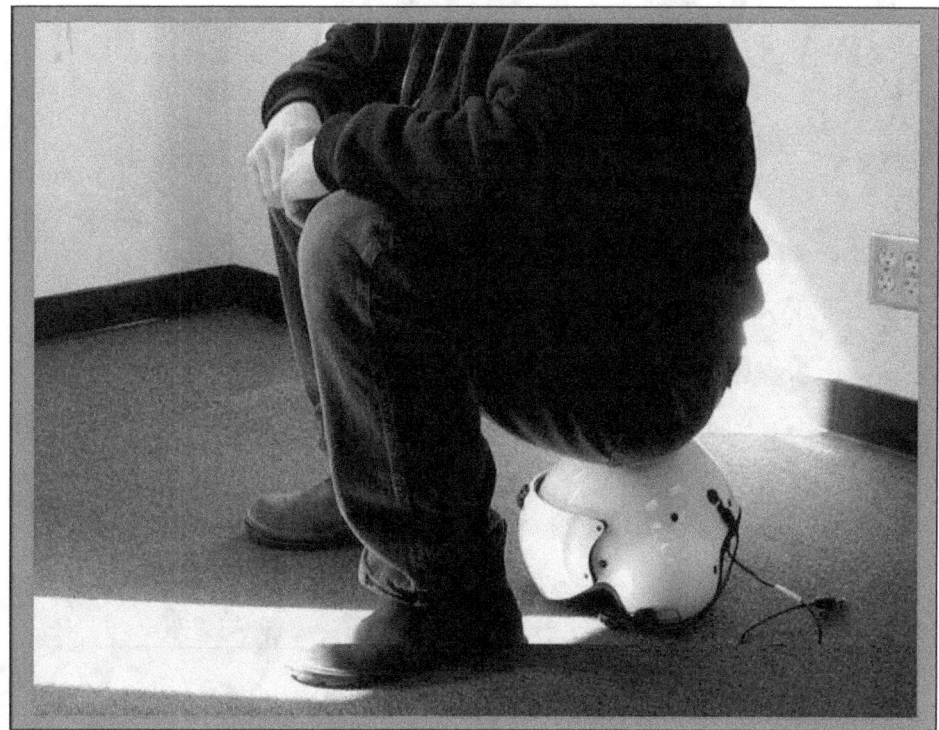

Most cracks in the helmet's shell are found on the ear cups, **don't** sit on your flight helmet.

How NOT to treat your flight helmet !!!

Too much heat can cook a flight helmet.

Keep your helmet clean, cool, and dry when not in use.

Who ya gonna call?

BLM Ramp Services, Boise, Idaho

National Interagency Fire Center
Attn: BLM Ramp Services
3833 S. Development Ave.
Boise, ID 83705

(208) 387-5529
(208) 387-5785 fax

helmets@nifc.blm.gov